The Alligator Book

THE ALLIGATOR BOOK

60 Questions & Answers

by William Bentley

illustrated by Barbara Wolff

Walker & Co. New York

DEDICATION

To my wife, Lois, and my two daughters Linda and Libby.

ACKNOWLEDGEMENT

I am grateful to Mike Fogarty and Jim Schortemeyer, wildlife biologists with the Florida Game and Fresh Water Fish Commission, and John Ogden, research biologist, Everglades National Park, for their valuable assistance.

Text Copyright © 1972 by William Bentley.
Illustrations Copyright © 1972 by Barbara Wolff.

All the characters and events portrayed in this story are fictitious.

First published in the United States of America
in 1972 by the Walker Publishing Company, Inc.

Published simultaneously in Canada by Fitzhenry & Whiteside, Limited, Toronto.

Trade ISBN: 0–8027–6115–1
Reinforced ISBN: 0–8027–6116–X

Library of Congress Catalog Card Number: 72–81375

Printed in the United States of America.

TABLE OF CONTENTS

What does an alligator look like?

An alligator looks like a giant lizard. It has a very long tail, huge jaws, sharp teeth, a rough hide, and short legs. An alligator floating on the water looks like a big log.

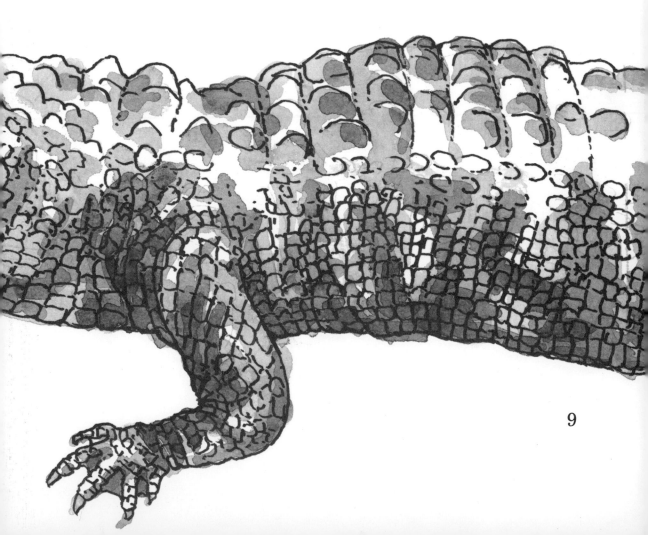

How did the alligator get its name?

When early Spanish explorers saw an alligator for the first time, they called out "El Largato," the Spanish word for lizard. Our word "alligator" comes from this term. The Seminole Indian name for the alligator is *allapattah*.

What is the alligator's scientific name?

Alligator mississippiensis
(miss-is-sip-pi-en-sis)

ALLIGATOR

SNAKE

What kind of animal is an alligator?

An alligator is a member of the reptile family. Reptiles are covered with scales, breathe through lungs, and are cold-blooded. Because it is cold-blooded, the alligator's body is the same temperature as the surrounding air or water.

12

TURTLE

LIZARD

13

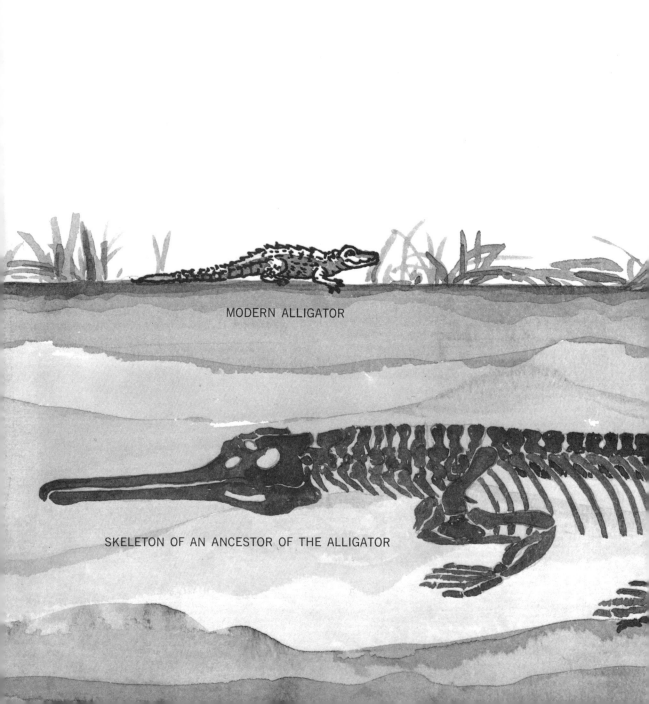

MODERN ALLIGATOR

SKELETON OF AN ANCESTOR OF THE ALLIGATOR

*Has the alligator changed much in the last
100 million years?*

The alligator today looks about the same as its ancestors did 137 million years ago except for its size. The ancestors of alligators once were much bigger—up to 60 feet long. They have lived on earth ever since the age of dinosaurs.

How does an alligator differ from a crocodile?

An alligator is darker and has a nose that is broader and blunter than a crocodile's. A crocodile has a tooth in the lower jaw that sticks up on each side when the crocodile closes its mouth. An alli-

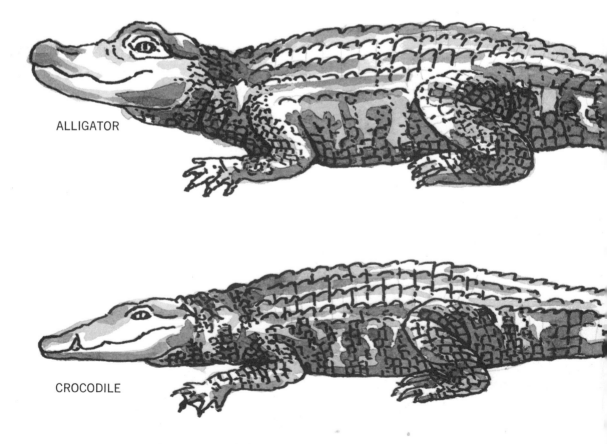

ALLIGATOR

CROCODILE

gator has such teeth, but you cannot see them stick up when the alligator closes its mouth. Alligators usually live in fresh water. The crocodiles in the United States are found in salt water.

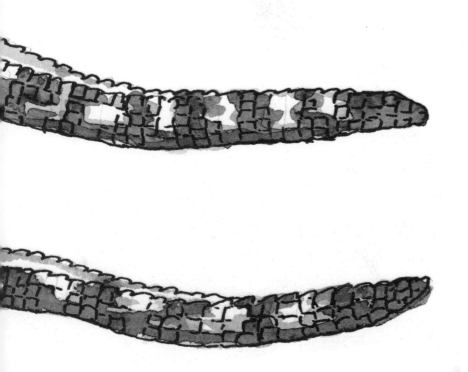

Where do American alligators live?

They live mostly in the southern and south-eastern part of the United States, particularly in Florida and Louisiana. They live in swamps, ponds, and slow-moving streams.

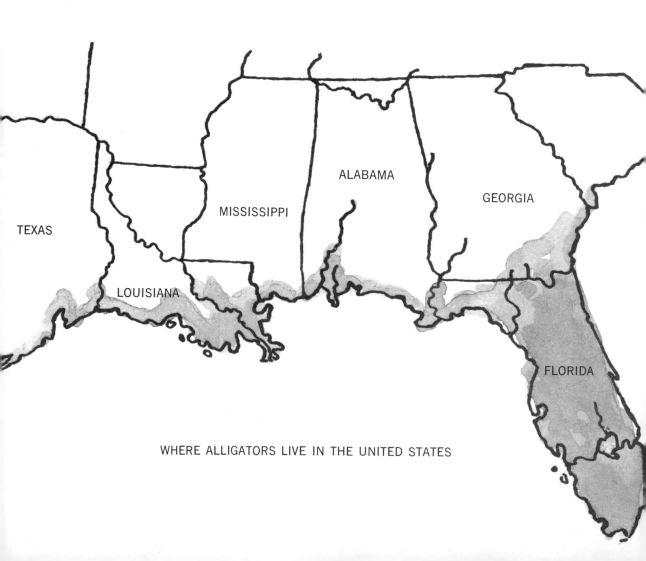

WHERE ALLIGATORS LIVE IN THE UNITED STATES

How long can an alligator live?

An alligator is considered to be old if it lives for twenty years, but one American alligator was recorded to have lived forty-six years.

Do alligators roam around or stay in one place?

Alligators have *territories* — places that they defend against other alligators. Male alligators have larger territories than females. Both male and female alligators make dens in the banks of a stream or pond. Or they may live in 'gator ponds.

What are 'gator ponds?

These are deep pools of water in which all vegetation has been cleared away by the alligator. The alligator does this by tearing out huge mouthfuls of plants with its jaws. A 'gator pond helps other wildlife, such as fish and birds, since it gives them a place to live and eat during the dry season.

20

Is an alligator strong?

Alligators are very strong. Their jaws are especially powerful. They can easily crush large turtle shells with their jaws.

Can a man wrestle with an alligator?

Yes. A man can easily hold an alligator's mouth shut with his hands. Once the jaws are closed, the alligator is flipped on its back. The blood goes to its small brain and causes it to black out.

How big can an alligator get?

One of the largest ever captured was 19 feet 2 inches long. However, a 12-foot alligator today is considered large.

How many species of alligators exist?

There are only two species of alligators, the American and Chinese alligator. The southeastern part of the United States and eastern China are the only places in the world where alligators can be found.

Does an alligator have the same type of skin all over its body?

No. Its back is covered with bony shields, while its underside has leathery scales.

Are alligators different colors?

The color depends upon the type of water in which an alligator lives. Those living in swamps are usually darker than those living in streams.

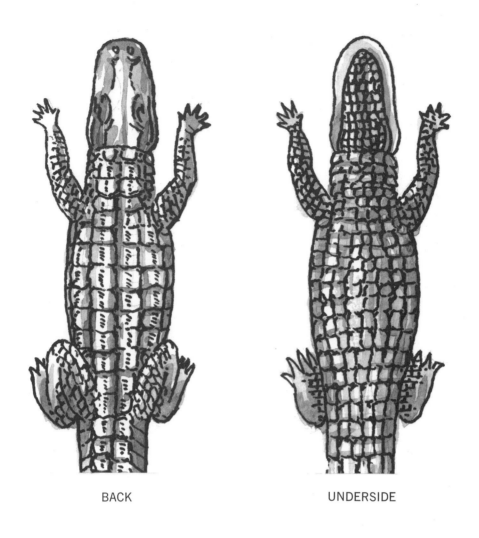

BACK   UNDERSIDE

Are male and female alligators different colors?

No. Their coloring is the same.

How well does an alligator see?

Like most reptiles, alligators have good vision. They see well at night. This is the time they usually search for food.

Does an alligator hear?

An alligator can hear very well with its small ears. They are located just back of its eyes and look like little half-moon shaped openings.

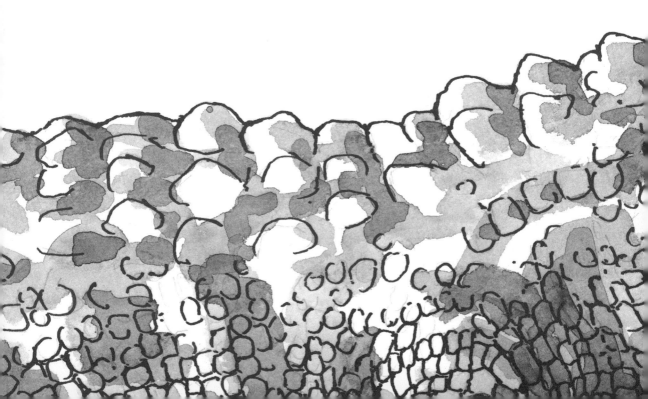

What protects an alligator's eyes and ears when it goes underwater?

The alligator is a natural fresh-water submarine. It can see underwater because it is equipped with a sort of third eyelid—a clear tissue that covers its eyes when it goes under the surface. It also has a flap of skin that covers its ears and keeps out the water.

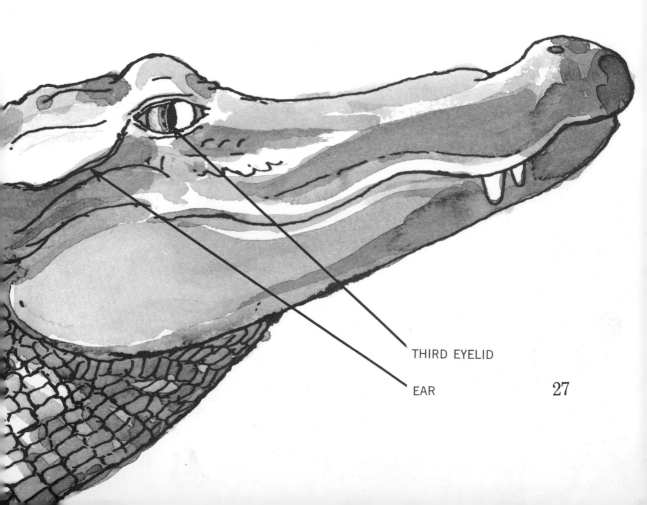

THIRD EYELID

EAR

27

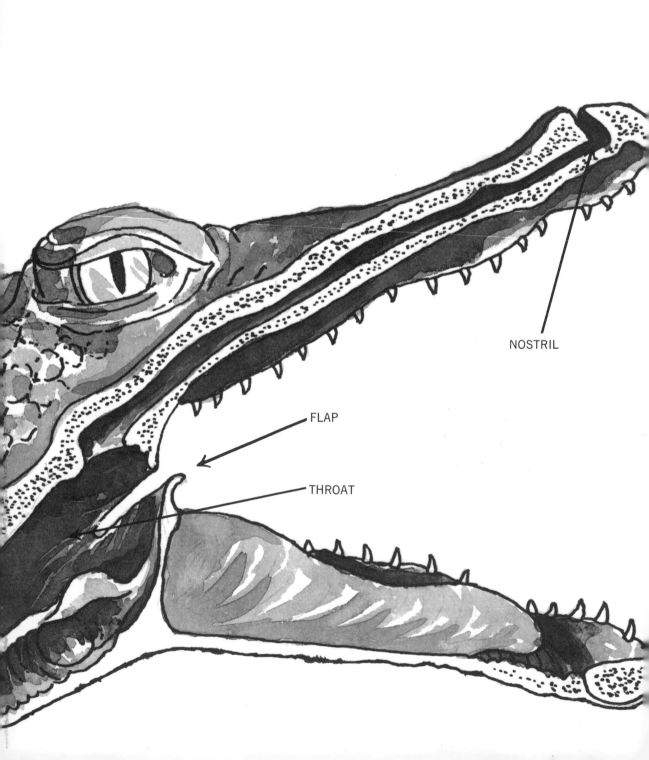

NOSTRIL

FLAP

THROAT

What kind of tongue does an alligator have?

The alligator's tongue is broad and thick. A flap at the back of its tongue prevents water from rushing down its throat when the alligator opens its mouth underwater.

What do alligators eat?

Alligators are animal eaters and their main food consists of snails, crayfish, shrimp, and crabs. They will also eat turtles, snakes, ducks, fish, and wading birds.

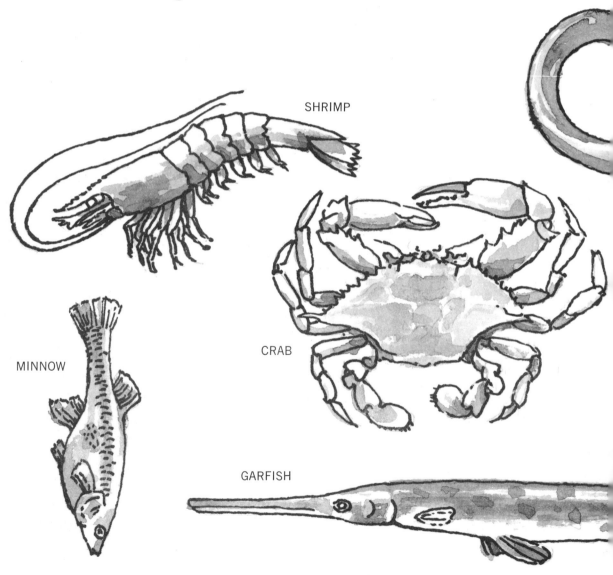

SHRIMP

CRAB

MINNOW

GARFISH

SNAKE

HERON

DUCK

SNAIL

TURTLE

31

How does an alligator catch its food?

The alligator grabs its prey with quick side swings of its head and with its jaws held partly open. Larger prey is pulled underwater and kept there until it drowns.

32

Can an alligator eat food underwater?

No. Although it often catches its food under-water, it must come to the surface to swallow it.

Does an alligator swallow its food whole?

Yes, it gulps its food down whole. But in the case of large prey, the alligator can use its jaws and teeth to break it up first. Then it swallows the meat in chunks. Powerful gastric juices dissolve the food when it reaches the alligator's stomach.

How powerful are the gastric juices in the alligator's stomach?

The gastric juices are powerful enough to dissolve bones, hair, and turtle shells.

How long can an alligator go without food?

This depends on the size of the alligator. The larger it is, the longer it can survive without food or water. Large alligators have been known to exist for months without food.

How does an alligator breathe?

The alligator breathes by inhaling and exhaling through lungs. It must breathe air by putting its nostrils, located on top of its nose, above water. Little flaps cover the alligator's nostrils underwater.

*How long can an alligator stay underwater
without drowning?*

An alligator needs very little oxygen and can
stay submerged for long periods of time, more than
an hour if necessary. However, like all lung-
breathers, it must eventually come to the surface
to breathe.

Why do alligators lie in the sun?

When they lie in the sun, they warm up. Also,
the sun and air help prevent fungus growth. The
ideal temperature for an alligator is 80°F to 90°F.

37

Does an alligator sleep?

Yes. When alligators sleep, they close their eyes just as people do. They sleep in the water as well as on land.

Is an alligator harder to see in the winter than the summer?

Yes. The air is usually colder than the water in winter. The alligator therefore stays in the water.

Is the alligator a slow-moving reptile?

An alligator is slow-moving when it is following its prey. But when it is in danger, it can move very fast.

How does the alligator use its legs in the water?

In the water, the alligator's legs help it to paddle and balance when floating for long periods of time.

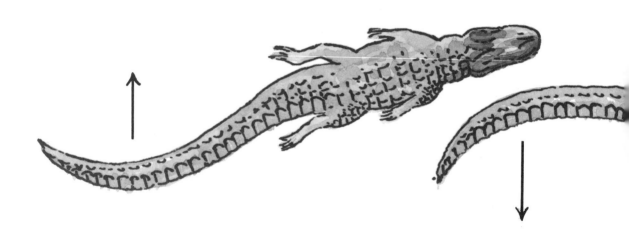

How does an alligator travel through water?

It holds its short legs close to its body and wags its powerful tail from side to side.

40

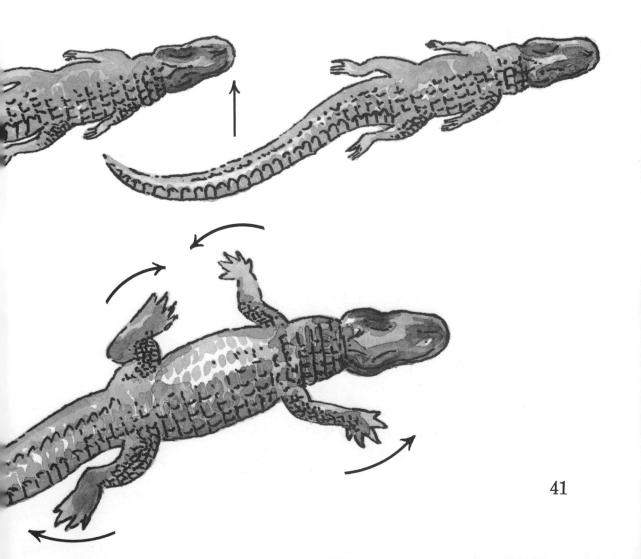

How does an alligator move on land?

It crawls on its short stumpy legs. This prevents it from dragging its huge body on the ground.

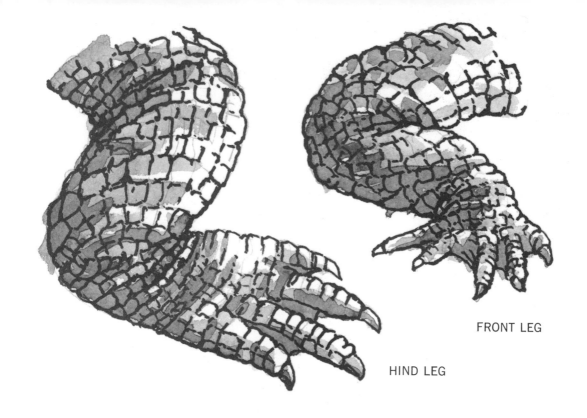

FRONT LEG

HIND LEG

Can an alligator move fast on land?

An alligator can run fast for short distances on land. However, it is more at home in the water and is a very rapid swimmer.

43

When do alligators mate?

They start to mate somewhere between the ages of five and six. The mating season is in the spring, and the mating occurs in the water.

How does a male alligator find a female?

In the spring the male alligator, or bull, roars loudly to establish his territory. The females answer the roars. In that way, the males find the females.

How do alligators mate?

Adult alligators ready to mate lie side by side in shallow water. The male alligator mounts the female alligator and ejects sperm into her body. There the sperm combines with the female's eggs or fertilizes them. The eggs can then develop into baby alligators. Before the fertilized eggs are laid, a shell is formed around each one.

*Where does the female alligator make her nest
and what does it look like?*

The female alligator builds her nest in her territory usually near the edge of her 'gator hole or pond. It is built on dry land. She gathers sticks, leaves, and water vegetation into a large mound, shaped like a cone. This is usually 3 feet to 7 feet across. She then hollows out a hole in the top of the nest with her back feet and deposits her eggs.

Will a female alligator use the same nest over again?

Not usually, but one female alligator was reported to have used the same nest for eight years.

How many eggs does the female alligator lay?

The female alligator usually lays about forty eggs, but the number of eggs can vary from twenty to sixty.

47

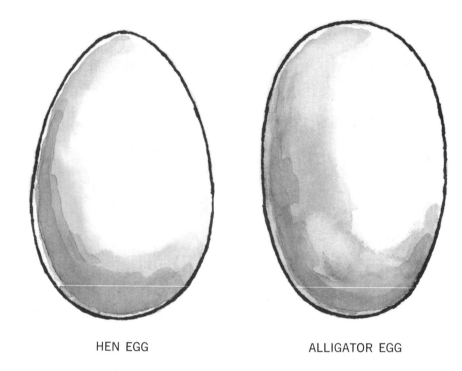

HEN EGG   ALLIGATOR EGG

How big are the eggs?

The eggs are about 3 inches long and 1 ¾ inches wide—a little bigger than large hen's eggs.

Does the female sit on her eggs, like a hen, to hatch them?

No, the heat of the sun, plus the heat from the rotting vegetation, incubate the eggs. They take about nine weeks to hatch.

How do the eggs hatch?

Much of the hard shell has broken away from the eggs when the eggs are ready to hatch. The young alligators move around actively and break the membrane left under the shell.

How big are baby alligators when they hatch?

Baby alligators are usually 9 inches long. Much of the baby alligator's length is in its tail. When the tail is wrapped around the baby alligator's body, it fits snugly into the egg.

49

How do the baby alligators get out of the nest?

Even before baby alligators hatch from the eggs, they start to make grunting noises. This is a signal to the mother alligator. She clears away the top and side of the nest and the baby alligators crawl out. Sometimes the baby alligators crawl out of the nest without the help of the mother.

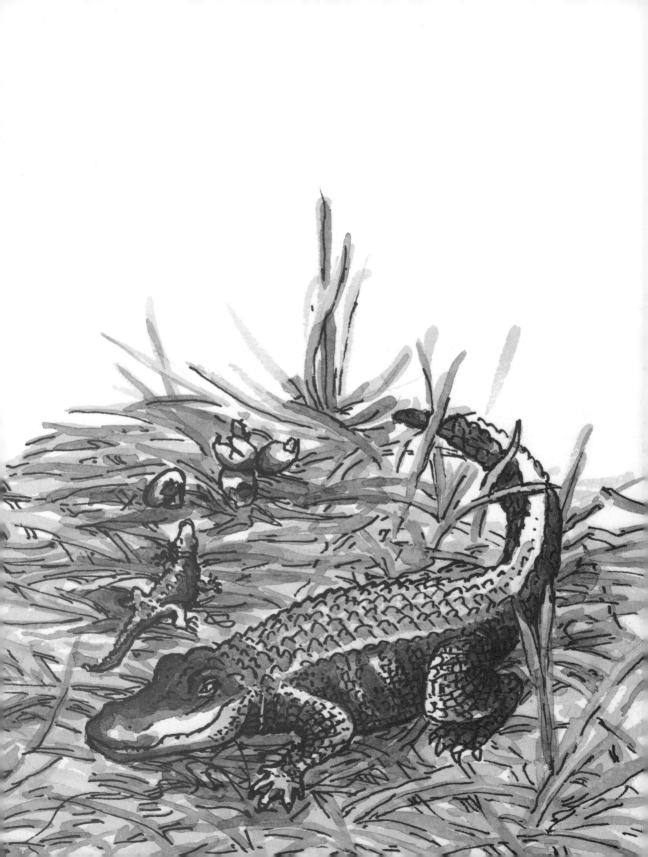

Does the mother alligator protect her young?

Yes. The mother alligator protects them for at least a year and often longer. When young alligators leave the nest, they head for nearby water. Some raccoons and wading birds catch baby alligators even though the mother alligator scares off many of these enemies by hissing loudly.

Do most baby alligators manage to get through their first year?

No. Many of them die.

Do male alligators grow faster than females?

They both grow about a foot a year during the first six years of life. Then the male grows faster than the female. After ten years, the male is about 9 feet long and weighs about 250 lbs. Females are usually 7 feet to 8 feet long and weigh over 165 lbs.

SIZE AT HATCHING

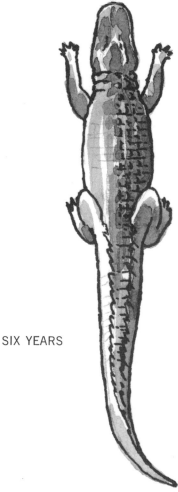

SIX YEARS

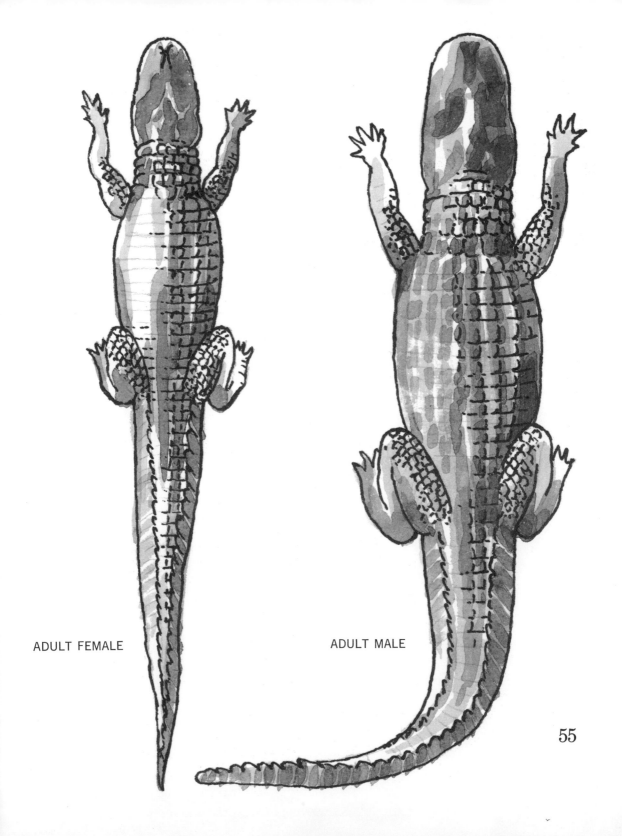

ADULT FEMALE

ADULT MALE

55

How do people catch alligators?

Alligators are usually hunted at night. Poachers, who hunt animals illegally, push their boats through the water as they prowl for alligators with a searchlight. An alligator's eyes shine like two red rubies when the light hits them. The

light also seems to hypnotize them. As a result, poachers can get very close. The poacher then either shoots the alligator between the eyes or hacks it behind the head with an ax.

What are alligator skins used for?

The skin from the stomach and sides of the alligator is used for making expensive leather goods such as luggage, shoes, wallets, and belts.

Why are alligators disappearing?

People are hunting alligators illegally because their hides are so valuable. Also, wetlands where alligators live are being drained for housing and commercial purposes.

Are alligators protected by laws?

Yes. In the states where alligators exist, very strict laws prohibit the killing of alligators for any purpose.

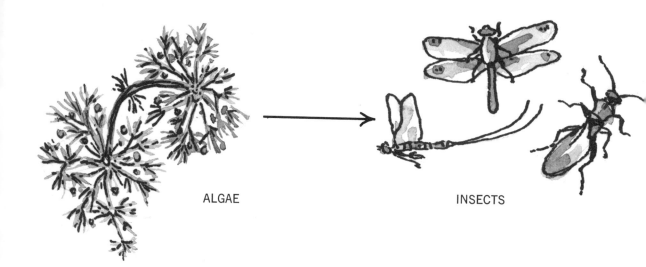

ALGAE   INSECTS

What part does the alligator play in the life-cycle of a swamp?

Water insects feed on the algae, which are simple water plants. Minnows eat the water insects. Frogs then eat the minnows. Big fish and snakes eat the frogs. Wading birds and small water animals eat big fish and snakes. Finally the alligator eats the birds and small water animals.

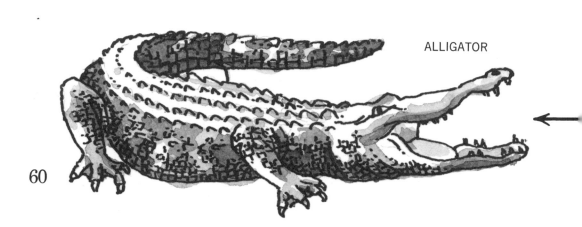

ALLIGATOR

60

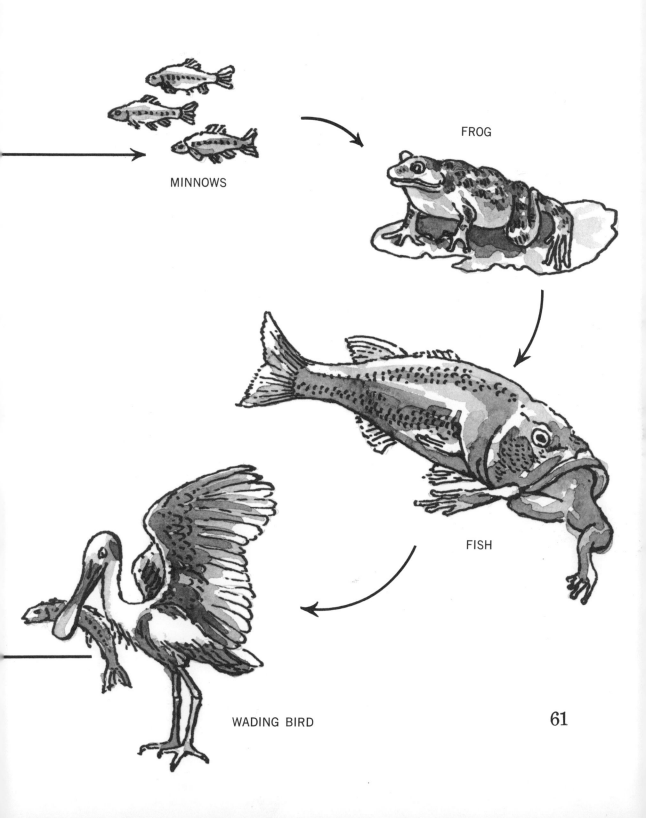

MINNOWS

FROG

FISH

WADING BIRD

61

Do alligators attack people?

Not usually. A wild alligator could hurt a person, but it is not as ferocious as commonly believed. Unless an alligator is cornered, it will usually move away. Bees kill more people than alligators.

What should a person do if he sees an alligator?

The best thing to do is keep a safe distance and leave the alligator alone.

Can baby alligators be kept as pets?

No. They are hard to feed and take care of and they usually die. It is against the law to sell them.

Why do we want to keep alligators in the world?

The alligator plays a vital and useful role in the balance of nature. The life-giving water found in 'gator ponds enables much wildlife to survive during a drought. Besides, the alligator is a very unusual and interesting reptile, one of our few remaining links with the pre-historic past.

ACKNOWLEDGEMENTS

The publisher is grateful for permission to use the following photographs:

Lynwood M. Chace from National Audubon Society, p. 36

Allan D. Cruickshank from National Audubon Society, pp. 18-19

Kit and Max Hunn from National Audubon Society, p. 58, p. 64

George Porter from National Audubon Society, p. 36